Thessalonians

BUILDING CHURCH IN CHANGING TIMES

CWR

Chris Leonard

Contents

Introduction

Did you know that there are documents concerning the beginnings of the very first Christian churches in Europe, that were written by eye-witnesses? Two of them date from just 20 or so years after Jesus died and one was written three years after those churches began. These letters still exist, giving us amazing insight into the gospel's transformative power. They also shed light on the life, personality and faith of the world-famous Christian missionary who wrote them. What's more, if you've ever flown to northern mainland Greece – holidayed in Halkidiki, for example – you probably landed at the airport of the still-important town to which he addressed the two documents.

You may have guessed I'm referring to 1 and 2 Thessalonians. I hope introducing them as I have will excite you about a few pages in a book that you may have read for years. Or perhaps you're just starting to explore the Bible and finding parts a bit obscure? The more I've looked into them, the more the two letters to the Thessalonians have excited me. How extraordinary that we can read church-building letters dating from the early 50s AD! Most scholars agree that, of all his letters still in existence, these are the very first the great apostle Paul wrote, unless Galatians snuck in first. If you're familiar with the Bible, you'll see how Paul later developed the phrases and trains of thought he wrote first in Thessalonians. In these earliest letters we see him discovering shiny new truths – particularly around how God built up new followers in their radically new faith. These two letters, simpler than many, lacking much systematic theology, are littered with uncut gems – look out for the recurring three: faith, hope and love.

At the time that Paul was writing, Thessalonica was a self-governing city under the Romans, capital of Macedonia and a busy port where the main east–west route from Byzantium to Rome met the road running north from the Aegean to the Danube. Imagine the comings and goings, the trading of goods and ideas, the lively mix of peoples and cultures, where free thought and 'free love' reigned.

First-century times, much like our own, were difficult and uncertain; huge changes were happening. As we'll see, Paul and his companions had only just planted the church when they had to flee the town. According to Acts 17 they'd stayed there a little over three weeks, though some references in Paul's letters suggest rather longer – he had time to find work (in the tent-making trade, see Acts 18:1–3) and received at least two lots of 'aid' from Philippi (Phil. 4:16).

Our first week's study focuses mainly on Paul's relationship with the Thessalonians and why he was writing to them. I won't repeat that here, except to mention that both letters say they are from Paul, Silas and Timothy, but most scholars agree Paul dictated them himself. The penultimate verse seems to bring us especially close to the man. 'I, Paul, write this greeting in my own hand, which is the distinguishing mark in all my letters. This is how I write' (2 Thess. 3:17). The penultimate verse of 1 Thessalonians answers something basic I asked when a child at school – how did a whole town read Paul's letters? 'I charge you before the Lord to have this letter read to all the brothers and sisters' (1 Thess. 5:27). Paul would have been writing to the smallish group in Thessalonica who had responded to his preaching and been adopted into Christ's family, as Paul himself had been earlier.

Before reaching the study in Week Two, sit down somewhere quiet and read both letters straight through. Panic not – together they contain only eight chapters and occupy just five pages in my Bible. You'll re-read them all,

and some several times, during this study. Parts remain obscure, so don't spend time now on what you don't understand. These are ancient documents. It's amazing how much we can learn about their context, cultures and events. The Holy Spirit will make clear anything else we need to know here and now. What the Thessalonians needed to know – there and then – is not our concern.

These letters aren't organised into long, systematic arguments for this or that, and so can appear slightly muddled. So we'll consider them, not chapter by chapter, but through themes, each looking at one or more building-tools for churches facing difficult or uncertain times. Tools that are as relevant to us today as they were then.

I pray that you might find Thessalonians as encouraging and up-building as I have done. That you'll see the power of the gospel at work in the midst of difficult circumstances. That you and your church will be further built up into God's 'living temple', with Christ as cornerstone – learning how to use the 'building tools' He gives more effectively. Some of these 'tools' are necessary for pulling down, but most – like encouragement, thanksgiving, prayer, faith, hope, love, holiness, the exercise of godly leadership and authority – build up. May they help you deal with difficult and contentious issues, with any misunderstandings that arise, with enemies and evil. May this study not be merely an intellectual exercise but, as with Paul's and the Lord's ministry to the Thessalonians, truly transformative, so that Jesus' good news will spread far and wide, to His glory. Amen!

WEEK 1

Beginnings: does the gospel work?

Opening Icebreaker

Tell the story of some seeds of the gospel that you've helped to plant. Did they grow and bear fruit quickly or slowly? Did 'germination' take years or fail altogether?

Bible Readings

- Acts 17:1–15 (key passage – the church's beginning in Thessalonica)
- Acts 16:9–40 (background events leading to the start of the Thessalonian church)
- Matthew 13:3–8, 18–23 (the parable of the sower)
- 1 Thessalonians 1:1–10 (Paul's visit to Thessalonica and what happened to them next)
- 1 Thessalonians 2:17–3:11 (Paul's longing to be with them again)

Opening Our Eyes

These readings set the context for Paul's short stay and subsequent 'relationship at a distance' with the fledgling church in Thessalonica. Acts 17:1–10 tells the story of how Paul arrived, preached and founded a little group of believers. But very soon he and his companions had to leave the town to which he later sent the particular letters we're studying in this study guide. It was as if they'd supervised the building of a small shack – could it survive and be built into a Temple of living stones?

Paul, Silas and Timothy's momentous visit to Thessalonica was short, perhaps only three weeks or so, and most likely happened in the summer of AD 50, only 17 years after Jesus died and rose again. A dramatic vision had called them from Asia Minor to Macedonia (now northern Greece). Yet Paul and his companions were hounded out of all three Macedonian towns where they'd preached the gospel and planted tiny new groups of believers. They'd had little time to teach the converts much about Jesus or life under His new covenant – and now these, the first European churches, were suffering persecution. Jesus had said that some gospel seeds that are planted in just such circumstances would die. What was going on?

Paul's letters to the Thessalonians are probably the very earliest letters of his that we have. One seems to follow quickly after the other and most scholars believe both were written from Corinth. Straight after being expelled from Thessalonica and Berea, Paul spent some time in Athens before continuing to Corinth, which means little time had passed after his short stay in Thessalonica – a year or two at most. No-one could have blamed him for being worried, disappointed, perhaps even questioning the Holy Spirit's guidance, yet he soon learns of the astounding hope, strong faith and genuine love thriving in the infant church he'd left so hurriedly.

Even though they were under persecution, these new-born lives showed the gospel's power at work. Because of them it was spreading far and wide. If Paul thought he'd left a half-completed shack, it had 'grown' into a series of small 'living temples'! Pause for a moment – rejoice in the amazing power of the gospel of Christ, as Paul did!

It's not easy, being a missionary. In my very first book, I write about the 'Church of Pentecost', the fastest-growing church in West Africa, which was founded by the missionary James McKeown. Back in 1945, during several setbacks, false starts and attacks, McKeown wrote that it must grieve God's heart to see His servants 'worrying about difficulties, pushing for results, interfering with that seed which can split rocks, open graves, unlock prison doors, give sight to the blind ... Oh the limitless power of that Word!'* Indeed the gospel has helped to overcome all of these difficulties and by 2013 the Church of Pentecost had over 12,500 churches in Ghana, involving eight per cent of the population – plus branches in 86 other countries!

We all, even Paul, worry and become discouraged at times. Let faith rise! I've been so encouraged by reading the story of the power of the gospel to transform the Thessalonians – and by hearing updates from the Church of Pentecost in West Africa. God works miracles to build His Church – yesterday, today and forever!

*Christine Leonard, *A Giant in Ghana* (Chichester, New Wine Press, 1989, p xiii) quoting James McKeown, in *Church of Pentecost, History of the Church of Pentecost* (Accra, Church of Pentecost, 1987).

Discussion Starters

1. How does Jesus' parable from Matthew 13 relate to the opening icebreaker question – and to this week's topic? What light does it throw on how the gospel works?

2. Paul was called to help spread the gospel in Macedonia, only to then be expelled from three of its towns. How do you imagine he felt?

3. How, and why, was the gospel spreading in and beyond Macedonia, according to 1 Thessalonians 1?

4. How did the brand new church build and deepen its faith, hope and love, according to our second reading from 1 Thessalonians?

5. What can you learn about those involved in church planting: a) from Paul and his companions, b) from the Holy Spirit and c) from the Thessalonians themselves?

_____

_____

_____

_____

_____

_____

6. Caring for people spiritually at a distance isn't easy, especially when the relationship – and faith – are so new. What can you learn from Paul's relationship with the Thessalonians and the way he communicates in his first letter?

_____

_____

_____

_____

_____

_____

7. What have you learnt about facing set-backs and difficulties in seeing the gospel established, or about Christian living and church-building in difficult times of change and upheaval?

_____

_____

_____

_____

_____

_____

Personal Application

Ask God to highlight for you a situation where you've been discouraged after sharing the gospel. Ask whether He's wanting to stir you up again to faith and action – maybe to write an email, a letter, or pick up the phone … somehow get in touch again? Perhaps you could re-establish links through someone else? Or simply pray again for those people and that place?

Seeing Jesus in the Scriptures

Like Paul, Jesus always seemed to be on the move. Sometimes great crowds responded to Him straightaway, but He had to discern whether they were simply after spectacular miracles or, like the Thessalonians, willing to follow Him down harder paths. Jesus brought in massive changes that, as with Paul later, led Him into conflict with the most religious of His countrymen. Yet it was the unlikely who were impelled to spread the gospel to those around them – for example the outcast woman at a Samaritan well who had the one conversation with Him (see John 4) and then evangelised her whole town. Others who might have been expected to respond, didn't – and some even set themselves against Him. Jesus wept over them but never gave up, even to the extent of giving His life.

WEEK 2

Building tools: encouragement and thanksgiving

Opening Icebreaker

Share some encouragement you've been given that made a difference, perhaps 'spring-boarding' you to dive into something you'd have hesitated to attempt otherwise. Or, if you have time and know each other reasonably well, try the idea suggested in the Leader's Notes.

Bible Readings

- 1 Thessalonians 1:2–10 (key passage)
- 2 Thessalonians 1:3–4 (shorter confirmation in the second letter)
- 1 Thessalonians 2:11–13 (Paul, the fatherly encourager – and thankfulness)
- 1 Thessalonians 4:9–10 (confirming encouragement about their love)
- 1 Thessalonians 5:11, 18 (encouragement to encourage – and be thankful)
- 2 Thessalonians 2:16–17 (God the encourager)

Opening Our Eyes

As suggested in the Introduction, I hope you've been able
to read both of Paul's letters to the Thessalonians through
in one sitting by now. What jumped out at you? For me
it was the sheer amount of encouragement Paul poured
out on this small group of new and persecuted Christians.
Clearly Paul was himself so encouraged by the amazing
growth of the life of Christ within this group. Indeed, in
1 Thessalonians 3:7–8 he writes, 'in all our distress and
persecution we were encouraged about you because of
your faith. For now we really live, since you are standing
firm in the Lord.' Imagine reading that about yourselves!
Imagine Paul calling you 'his glory and joy' as he did
the Thessalonians: 'For what is our hope, our joy, or the
crown in which we will glory in the presence of our Lord
Jesus when he comes? Is it not you?' (1 Thess. 2:19–20).

Paul begins nearly all his letters with encouragement and
recognition of Jesus' life in the people to whom he writes,
even when he has to deal with problems, or sin, later. He
is always realistic – he doesn't wear rose-tinted spectacles
through which he can see only good things. That he
notices some of Jesus' qualities evident and growing in
people – and tells them so – can only build them up. It
encourages him, them (and us) and brings glory to God.
Psychologists say that praising – and modelling – the
good is normally more effective at changing people's
behaviour for the better, than criticising and prohibiting
the bad. The very word 'encouragement' means 'putting
courage into'. Let's agree to do it more often – and always
before we think of criticising!

Paul even boasts about the Thessalonians. I thought
boasting was not a desirable trait, but Paul does not boast
about himself: instead he tells everyone about the power
of God at work in them. It has the opposite effect from
running a person or group down. While negative gossip

is destructive: positive 'gossip' about the good news of changed lives helps Jesus' message spread, and brings glory to Him.

If encouragement can change, build up and enable, so can an attitude of thankfulness. I find it easy to slip into cynicism and 'grumble mode' – about the state of the world and more or less anything that dwells therein! In effect that means that I forget about God – for it's His world!

On reaching near burn-out after two terrible years of one bad thing in our family happening after another, I came to expect that, when I emerged from one dark 'tunnel', more darkness would loom ahead. I could see no end to it. Then I remembered a book someone had recommended. *One Thousand Gifts* is Ann Voskamp's earthed yet transcendent account of rising to the challenge of listing a thousand things she loves.[*] If it sounds over-optimistic, it isn't. Through tragedies and gruelling times she discovered spiritual principles like 'thankfulness precedes the miracle' – think of Gospel stories like the feeding of the 5,000. Following her example changed my attitude and contributed to my healing. Then, at various low points, six people who knew nothing of the situation 'randomly' phoned or emailed encouragement for things I'd done in the past – and forgotten! I'd been feeling useless but the timing demonstrated their – and God's – care and affirmation, bringing the beginnings of new hope, comfort and courage – things we all need to build faith in difficult, changing times.

[*]Ann Voskamp, *One Thousand Gifts* (Grand Rapids, Zondervan, 2010).

Discussion Starters

1. In what ways do you and your church need building up? Do you allow God, and people, to encourage you?

   _____
   _____
   _____
   _____
   _____

2. Make a list of the things that Paul thanked God for or encouraged the Thessalonians about. Notice how specific he was. How can you be more specific in your encouragement of and thankfulness for others?

   _____
   _____
   _____
   _____
   _____

3. If we're made in God's image there are treasures inside all of us. Can you ask God to reveal the treasures within people who irritate or even hurt you? Pray and thank God for them, see Jesus in them and ask for wisdom as to how to tell them the good you see.

   _____
   _____
   _____
   _____
   _____
   _____

4. How might you change conversations from negative to positive 'gossip'? Or tell stories of God-changed lives and situations, in everyday language?

_____

_____

_____

_____

_____

5. How might it work to 'thank God continually' (1 Thess. 2:13) and 'give thanks in all circumstances' (1 Thess. 5:18)?

_____

_____

_____

_____

_____

6. Are you being prompted to encourage someone undergoing persecution – write letters perhaps? Or to encourage someone who's suffering – for example from illness, loss, depression or a sense of helplessness?

_____

_____

_____

_____

_____

7. How can you encourage your church leaders? And seekers or new Christians?

_____

_____

_____

_____

_____

Personal Application

Make a note of how God is encouraging you right now. If you don't know, ask Him! Then set about completing any actions you wrote in response to the discussion starters, on a regular basis.

Seeing Jesus in the Scriptures

Jesus always drew near and encouraged people, even if correction had to come later. Think of Him naming His fickle, impulsive, jumping-to-wrong-conclusions disciple, Simon, 'the rock on which I will build my church.' (Matt. 16:18). What did Jesus see in Simon? Was His encouragement prophetic in the sense of 'true of the future only' or did Jesus see potential hidden at the time, part of the image of God capable of growing within? Gems hidden beneath layers of a tough life as a fisherman, or even buried beneath the raw grief of a bereaved young husband? (Peter had a mother-in-law but we hear nothing of his wife.)

Building on what kind of leadership and authority?

Opening Icebreaker

This week, try singing or reading the words of Graham Kendrick's well-known hymn *The Servant King*, or share examples of good and bad use of authority and leadership outside of the church – during your school days or at work, for example. What made them good or bad? What effect did they have on you and others?

Bible Readings

- Philippians 2:5–13 (Jesus' attitude as our example)
- 1 Thessalonians 2:1–14 (key passage)
- 1 Thessalonians 2:17–3:11 (reminder of a relevant passage read in Week 1)
- 2 Thessalonians 3:1–18 (Paul's passions, vulnerability and authority as leader)
- 2 Thessalonians 1:11–12 (a leader's prayer and vision for his flock)

Opening Our Eyes

When I moved home and church to take up my first job after university, one of the first Bible studies we did in the small home group I joined was on 'what can a flock expect of its leader, and vice versa?' Good question! Paul's letters to the Thessalonians reveal some helpful answers.

What kind of power and authority does a church need from its leaders, especially when going through times of difficulty, change or growth? The simple answer of course is 'the kind that is in Christ Jesus', which is why I chose a famous passage from Philippians as our first reading. I have met a handful of people in Christian leadership of one kind or another who have carried His paradoxical mix of humility and authority long-term. Not perfectly of course, none of us is perfect, but enough to give me real insight into what Jesus must have been like as a leader on earth and what His rule and reign – that is, His kingdom – is all about. It's a compelling mix. I can see why the disciples gave up everything to follow such a One.

The purpose of this study is not to provide ammunition for criticising our own church leaders for any failure to come up to Paul's, let alone Christ's, standards. But learning from Paul as well as Jesus might help us to pray with more understanding for our leaders – and for all those amongst us who are exercising leadership of any type, at any level. We have an unusually close encounter with Paul in these two early letters of his. They reveal a lot about the kind of leader he was, including on an emotional level. He writes like a parent agonising over absent and vulnerable children. We see Paul's own vulnerability – for example to lies, misunderstandings and trouble-makers, both within and outside the church. We see his needs – basic ones like food and shelter, means of communication, for money to do his work and to travel onwards.

He needed others' prayers – and those who would listen and recognise his God-given authority – a Christian leader can't make people follow! We see Paul's authenticity, his dependence on Christ, his concern that all glory went to Him. We see his love – unconditional yet not weak, self-giving, others-serving – a gut-wrenching love that reminds us so much of Jesus.

We also see the way Paul dealt with misunderstandings. As a leader of new churches he battled theological errors and was challenged about his own words, actions and motives. We'll look more closely at this another week. Remember that Paul had been forced to leave the vulnerable new church at Thessalonica without establishing a local leadership or even those who could teach. Many of the problems revealed in other parts of his letters may well have resulted from these lacks. Thank God the church had the Holy Spirit!

From these two short letters, their context within Acts and other letters of Paul, we can gain further insight into how he spotted and trained up potential new leaders, like young Timothy. Without this approach being brought forward in successive generations, churches will die. If you would like to find out more about this, read the Leader's Notes for this week.

Discussion Starters

1. What qualities of a good leader do you find in Paul's letters to the Thessalonians?

2. In what ways did he model life within the new covenant to them?

3. What drove Paul? Where did his authority – and humility – spring from? And his vision for the Thessalonians?

4. How did Paul lead – and communicate – from a distance?

5. Reading between the lines of both letters, in what ways would you imagine that at least some people in Thessalonica were challenging or undermining Paul's authority? How did he deal with these people and issues?

_____

_____

_____

_____

6. How and why were Paul's expectations of the Thessalonians let down – and theirs of him?

_____

_____

_____

_____

7. Paul tells the Thessalonians to obey him. That kind of authority doesn't always sit easily in today's independent culture. And power is easy to abuse. When might it be right not to obey leaders? How might we know when we're being led astray? (These are huge, important questions. Tackle them only if you've time and feel discussing them would be helpful.)

_____

_____

_____

_____

8. From what we learn of Timothy here and in other parts of Scripture mentioned in the Leader's Notes for this week, what can we learn of how Paul trained the next generation of leaders?

_____

_____

_____

_____

Personal Application

Pray for the leaders of your church and think of practical ways in which you might offer to serve them. Pray for any church situations you know of where there's fragmentation or contention among the leadership or congregation, or indeed between the leadership of different churches within a locality. Pray for godly leaders to be brought forward from the next generation and consider whether you can help to recognise and mentor any.

Seeing Jesus in the Scriptures

Jesus is the ultimate head of the Church, a mighty yet humble Servant-King whose name is Love. His leadership style isn't often seen within our culture, yet in the Gospels we see Him washing His disciples' feet, constantly reaching out to those considered beyond the pale within religious or secular society, turning the outcasts, the weak and vulnerable into His most ardent followers. Think of Mary Magdalene or Matthew the tax collector. Think also of the way Jesus asserted His authority – by His discourse in the Temple at the age of twelve, by teaching and healing, by doing only what He saw the Father doing, by walking dumb as a sheep to the slaughter, then rising again and ascending in glory and – by doing all that without sin – pioneering the way through death and making straight the way to God for all of us.

WEEK 4

Prayer and the nature of salvation

Opening Icebreaker

In a couple of sentences (without too much detail) share what kind of conversations you've had with God this week. Were they mainly thanks and praise, urgent requests for yourself or others, grumbles, or something else?

Bible Readings

- John 17:1–26 (Jesus' long prayer for Himself, His disciples and all believers)
- 1 Thessalonians 1:2–5 (Paul's prayer)
- 1 Thessalonians 3:9–13 (Paul's prayer)
- 1 Thessalonians 5:8–10, 16–24 (working out our salvation)
- 2 Thessalonians 1:11–12 (Paul's prayer)
- 2 Thessalonians 2:13–3:5 (working out our salvation; Paul's prayer requests)

Opening Our Eyes

Reading through Thessalonians in preparation for this study, I made a list of the verses that stood out to me as real gems. Many of them are worth learning by heart! As I look back over that list, I notice many of the verses are either prayers or about prayer, including Paul's requests for prayer. Altogether we get an amazing insight into a major building-tool – his prayer life. If the letters show us one side of his conversation with the Thessalonians, perhaps his prayers show us one side of his relationship with God – the relationship that links Paul with them, although he can't be in Thessalonica.

The Scottish Highlands have many single-track 'A' roads with passing places. The road-widenings are marked by little signs on posts, so a driver can look ahead and judge whether they or the on-coming vehicle should pull over. God kept nudging me about those signs. It took a while for me to understand their significance. I eventually saw that any time we meet with a person can be a 'passing place'. We may share a 'passing place' with a person for decades, or a few seconds in a supermarket queue. Our meetings with God are also 'passing places'. Especially, perhaps, at particular times in our lives where His manifest presence makes prayer easy. But when God is in the encounters between two or more people sharing a 'passing place', something special happens. As our time meets His eternity, salvation and redemption are present.

In Thessalonians, many of Paul's prayers are for their salvation – where God and humanity meet. He may not have had time to explain salvation fully to them – he says he longs to supply what is lacking in their faith. That's why he prays to God, who is present with him in Corinth and them in Thessalonica. He tells them what he is praying for very specifically. Salvation is, after all 'the word of God, which is indeed at work in you who believe' (1 Thess. 2:13). It's not Paul's words or work, it's God's. All the glory is to and for Him. So it's not wrong to rejoice in and thank Him for what you can see of your own 'work produced by faith, your labour prompted by love, and your endurance inspired by hope in our Lord Jesus Christ' (1 Thess. 1:3). Recognise too that the gospel may arrive in particular passing places, 'not simply with words but also with power, with the Holy Spirit and with deep conviction' (1 Thess. 1:5).

Prayer is a two-way conversation. God speaks to us through many means, not least through prophecies. Paul urges 'Do not treat prophecies with contempt' – though of course one needs to 'test them all' (1 Thess. 5:20–21). Our part in prayer involves intercession – plus lots of blessing others, if Paul's practice in all of his letters means anything! It is very important to praise God in prayer and give 'thanks in all circumstances'. In week two, I mentioned Ann Voskamp discovering the spiritual principle that 'thanksgiving precedes miracle'. Paul and Silas experienced just that in Philippi after they had been flogged, thrown into prison and shackled – they were 'praying and singing hymns to God, and the other prisoners were listening to them.' That's when an earthquake struck. Rather than it causing death and destruction, the doors 'flew open' and 'everyone's chains came loose'. Powerful stuff, enabling them to continue their mission in Thessalonica. No wonder Paul says 'Do not quench the Spirit' (1 Thess. 5:19).

Discussion Starters

1. Compare the Lord's prayer (Matt. 6:5–8 or Luke 11:1–13) and/or John 17 with Paul's prayer (see the Leader's Notes). What essentials do both parties pray for? How? Why? Do your prayers match theirs?

2. How can we 'pray continually'?

3. Paul (and Jesus) knew converts would suffer persecution, difficulties, divisions and misunderstandings. How might you pray more effectively for the suffering church today? And for divided churches or those 'going off the rails' somehow?

4. Reading between the lines, identify places where Paul's extraordinary faith, peace, joy and prayer life were less consistently super-human than we sometimes imagine. Discuss parallels with your expectations for yourselves. How do you find God's grace?

5. Might you ask God for specifics when praying? If appropriate, do you tell the people you're praying for what they are?

----

6. What do our readings reveal about salvation – who makes it happen, what's it saving people from, where does it lead, who/what is it for? Ask God to show you how 'the word of God [is] at work in you who believe' – and to make Himself known in your 'passing places'.

----

7. Do you ever 'quench the spirit' through indifference or opposition, stifling God's empowering Word or treating prophecy with contempt? Why?

Look out!.
Relate where a passing - place
has happened + what happened

Personal Application

There is so much you could do to apply this week's teachings to your life. You can deepen aspects of your prayer life; expand your own ability to be honest with God and receive His grace, His power, His Word, His guidance, His Spirit. Explore more about blessing others; explore the fullness of what salvation means and how God might be signposting particular 'passing places' where you, as a group or individual, could meet others and begin to open their eyes to His presence, so that they can find salvation too.

Seeing Jesus in the Scriptures

Read John 17 again. Meditate on it as though you were there, hearing Jesus pray it Himself before His crucifixion. Ask Him to speak to you this week. Do the same with the prayer Jesus taught His disciples to say, reading it in the context of His teaching on prayer (Matt. 6:5–18 and/or Luke 11:1–13).

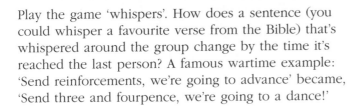

WEEK 5

Dealing with difficult or contentious issues and misunderstandings

Opening Icebreaker

Play the game 'whispers'. How does a sentence (you could whisper a favourite verse from the Bible) that's whispered around the group change by the time it's reached the last person? A famous wartime example: 'Send reinforcements, we're going to advance' became, 'Send three and fourpence, we're going to a dance!'

Alternatively, you could consider how you've dealt with being misunderstood in word or behaviour.

Bible Readings

- 1 Thessalonians 2:1–12 (clearing up misunderstandings about Paul)
- 1 Thessalonians 4:13–18 (clarifying what happens when Christians die)
- 1 Thessalonians 5:1–6, 9–10 (clarifying Jesus' second coming)
- 2 Thessalonians 2:1–12 (more clarification about the future)
- 2 Thessalonians 3:6–14 (following Paul's clear example)
- Matthew 24 (optional – Jesus' words about the future)

Opening Our Eyes

We've seen Jesus' powerful gospel quickly transforming those who became Christians in Thessalonica in many important ways – but not all. With so few weeks' teaching and opportunity to learn from Paul about this new faith, no wonder misunderstandings arose. Naturally people would argue and become confused about the finer points of theology and of the future when they hadn't heard the full story! There are twentieth-century examples of when sudden war or revolution forced missionaries to leave before they'd taught the new believers much. With only snippets of Scripture in their language, in one place they were literally cutting off/out their sinful hands and eyes, thinking to follow Jesus' command in Matthew 5:29–30. Or exterminating dogs, as one passage used the word 'dog' to indicate an evil or unclean person.

Perhaps some Thessalonians, feeling Paul had abandoned them, began to doubt both the man and his teachings. Mistrust and lies, when allowed to thrive, can tear a church down. With only Paul's side of the correspondence, we don't know exactly what went on, but we can gain insight into how he dealt with the situation.

Paul and his team had not had occasion to answer the pressing questions that had arisen since their visit. The Thessalonian Christians hadn't expected any of their number to die before Jesus returned. Now some had – where exactly were they? How should they mourn them? The Early Church expected Jesus to return very soon. Jesus said, 'For the Son of Man is going to come in his Father's glory with his angels, and then he will reward each person according to what they have done. Truly I tell you, some who are standing here will not taste death before they see the Son of Man coming in his kingdom' (Matt. 16:27–28).

This still puzzles me and others. Although two millenia have passed since Jesus died and rose again, Paul's instructions to the Thessalonians to be prepared for His return are just as relevant, if not more so.

School science lessons teach that electrons circle the nucleus of atoms as planets circle the sun. I can picture that! Older students learn that this model doesn't fully fit the facts. My non-scientific brain can't grasp the new explanations. I can only wonder at the unimaginable complexities of the universe and sub-atomic particles alike. But not even celebrity physicist Brian Cox can hope to understand the immensity, the eternity, the complexity and simplicity, the 'otherness' of God. So what is eternal life in all its fullness like? Stuck in time, in a fallen world, we see only in part. What will the new heavens and earth be like, or life after we die? Scripture uses picture-language that, like Nobel Prize winning physicist Niels Bohr's over-simplistic model of the atom, doesn't offer full explanations.

Paul, struggling to correct a misapprehension, appears to contradict some of his words from the first Thessalonians letter in the second. We may well ask: 'When will Jesus come again and what's all this about meeting Him in the air?' Or, 'Who's the "Man of Lawlessness" and who "restrains" him?' Theories abound and people love to argue about them. In Bible times they also argued about 'endless genealogies' (1 Tim. 1:4), numerology, and whether God could make something so big He couldn't lift it.

When Christians have different views surrounding the return of the Lord Jesus Christ it is important to show respect to others whilst at the same time trying to understand the essentials of what the Bible says. Above all, concentrate instead on Jesus – wonder, worship, faith, hope and love!

Discussion Starters

1. How does Paul address misunderstandings about his own motives and behaviour? Who else in the Bible had to deal with this kind of issue? How might all this inform your own actions and reactions in similar circumstances?

   _____

   _____

   _____

   _____

   _____

   _____

   _____

2. What can you learn about reactions, grieving and hope when Christians close to us die?

   _____

   _____

   _____

   _____

   _____

   _____

   _____

3. What difference does it make to know that Jesus is coming again, to see His work completed and evil finally vanquished in a new heaven and a new earth?

   _____

   _____

   _____

   _____

   _____

   _____

   _____

4. Have you ever been unsettled or alarmed by some prophecy, report or letter purporting to come from a man or woman of God? Or been gripped yourself by some lie or delusion? What can you learn from Thessalonians about how to handle such things?

_____

_____

_____

_____

_____

_____

5. How might you teach new Christians – and/or children – the essentials of our faith and how to build on them?

_____

_____

_____

_____

_____

6. How does Paul – and your church – handle controversy and contentious issues? In your community, what do these things centre around today? Are any issues like the elephant in the room – too big and scary to mention? How do you seek God humbly together?

_____

_____

_____

_____

_____

_____

Personal Application

Pray for wisdom and then pursue whatever God highlights for you from this week's study concerning preventing or stopping anything destructive and beginning to re-build.

Seeing Jesus in the Scriptures

Jesus spent a lot of time dealing with contentious issues and misunderstandings. Consider how He did this when dealing with different groups such as the Pharisees, 'ordinary' Jews, Samaritans, Romans and others. He would refuse to involve Himself in 'silly' discussions over matters such as who is married to whom in heaven, a question they'd asked to make a point about whether the Pharisees or the Sadducees were right about life after death (Matt. 22:23–33). Notice how Jesus showed they hadn't grasped the basics, like God 'is not the God of the dead but of the living'. He was said to speak with 'wisdom' and 'authority'. At other times He kept silent, letting His actions, or His suffering, speak. He'd provoke questions – or ask them right back. He'd tell stories both to illuminate and to challenge – see Matthew 13:13.

Jesus instructed His disciples to: 'be as shrewd as snakes and as innocent as doves … when they arrest you, do not worry about what to say or how to say it. At that time you will be given what to say, for it will not be you speaking, but the Spirit of your Father speaking through you' (Matt. 10:16,19–20). In other words, don't follow a formula. Jesus has given us brains to use and a living relationship with Father, Son and Holy Spirit to look to, just as He Himself did, when faced with contentious issues or misunderstandings!

WEEK 6

Dealing with persecution, enemies and evil

Opening Icebreaker

Discuss what each of you look for in the ending of a story or novel – and why. Do you prefer 'happily ever after' endings? Ones with everything finished neatly? Do you check out the ending early on, sneaking a peek at the last pages or at 'spoilers' on the internet?

Bible Readings

- 1 Thessalonians 2:1–2 (telling the gospel in spite of strong opposition)
- 1 Thessalonians 2:13–3:8 (opposition from the Jews, Satan, persecution)
- 2 Thessalonians 1:3–11 (perseverance, faith, strength, judgment from God)
- 2 Thessalonians 2:3–17 ('man of lawlessness' – dealing with delusions)
- 2 Thessalonians 3:2–3 (God's protection)
- 2 Corinthians 11:24–28 (Paul facing enemies, persecution, suffering, evil)

Opening Our Eyes

Not many people read to be depressed! Writers' manuals say nearly everyone expects some hope at the end of even the darkest, most tragic story. Plus some kind of change and resolution, though maybe not all ends tied up neatly, nor all problems resolved. I believe it's central to the way God made us that faith, hope and love 'remain' (1 Cor. 13:13). We're built to need hope in real life, especially when facing trials and conflicts. So, when we 'rehearse' them through fictional characters, though mid-story things may look terrible, hope remains part of the 'contract' of what we expect.

Not all ends are tied up neatly in terms of what happened to the Thessalonians, nor about God's future end-game for any of us. We're not sure exactly what Paul meant by some of the things he wrote about in approximately AD 50. Nevertheless, what was true for the Thessalonians, facing some degree of persecution and a lot of change and uncertainty, is still true for us now. The most important thing to keep in mind is that, as Christians, we're on the winning side. Faith, hope and love remain, and will fill everything and everyone because Christ will come again in triumph, to reign fully and forever.

Meanwhile we live amidst all kinds of suffering and conflict, just as characters often do throughout a novel – it's how they grow! Our own internal conflicts make us vulnerable to sin, betrayal, giving up in despair ... We may experience conflicts with the forces of evil and the 'powers that be' simply because we are following Jesus. But He gives us hope, and that hope is real. He's revealed at least the gist of the story's ending!

The Thessalonians faced some degree of persecution, we're not sure exactly what. It appeared to come mainly from local Jews. They seemingly felt threatened by this new message that Paul and Silas had been preaching in their synagogue, converting mainly Gentiles who attended. You'll remember how these Jews told the city officials how Paul was stirring up trouble: 'defying Caesar's decrees, saying there is another king' (Acts 17:6–8). A person wouldn't survive being 'severely flogged' very often, as Paul and Silas had been so recently in Philippi (Acts 16:23). That's why the Thessalonian and then the Berean Christians had them spirited out of their cities when trouble threatened. If Paul couldn't return to Macedonia until Acts 20, presumably it still wasn't safe. We know he had to rely on young Timothy for news and messages, who had been able to stay under the radar and avoid both flogging and imprisonment. We can gain a lot of insight into how Paul dealt with persecution, enemies and evil – and from how he advised new Christians to act under those circumstances.

Discussion Starters

1. Who or what are the enemies in today's Bible readings? What form does their enmity take? How and to what degree does all this relate to your experiences as a Christian?

    _____

    _____

    _____

    _____

    _____

    _____

    _____

2. From today's Bible readings, list the 'tools' to withstand enemies, evil and suffering. Share any you've seen working in your life. You might like to add a scripture that has helped when you've faced suffering, injustice, evil and so forth.

    _____

    _____

    _____

    _____

    _____

    _____

3. What are God's strategies for dealing with opposition and evil day by day? Who holds back lawlessness, then and now (2 Thess. 2:7)?

    _____

    _____

    _____

    _____

    _____

4. Do these statements remind you of anything in the Old Testament? a) People who do not yet 'heap up their sins to the limit' (1 Thess. 2:16). b) God sending delusions (2 Thess. 2:11–12)? How might understanding these scriptures help us to pray about situations involving evil or persecution today?

_____

_____

_____

_____

_____

_____

_____

5. What have you learned from Thessalonians about God's ultimate strategy and the 'end' of our story?

_____

_____

_____

_____

_____

_____

6. What is meant by God's wrath, and how is it reconciled with His love? Who, in the end, will suffer it?

_____

_____

_____

_____

_____

_____

_____

Personal Application

What difference will an increased understanding of the
sweep of 'God's story' make to the way you live? How
will it help you to deal with suffering and evil, and with
those who work against you – and Him? Pray about how
to lay better hold on some of the tools or 'equipment' He
offers in the scripture you've looked at this week.

Seeing Jesus in the Scriptures

Jesus' wrath seemed directed almost entirely against
those who kept others from knowing His Father. These
included some religious leaders who excluded so many
from God's house, pronouncing them unfit to enter
His presence, who made the Law ever more elaborate
and impossible to keep, doctrine more obscure and
intellectual knowledge mandatory. On the other hand,
Jesus didn't shun meeting evil head on – for example,
during His temptations in the wilderness.

In Gethsemane and on the cross, Jesus faced persecution,
enemies and all kinds of trials and suffering meekly,
knowing He was in His Father's will, knowing that
this was how He would redeem people back into the
relationship God had always intended, letting His Father
be the judge rather than trying to defend Himself. Jesus
tried explaining many times to His disciples that He must
die, rise, ascend to the Father and come again, but they
didn't understand. We understand the first three of these
promises better than those first disciples, for they are in
our past. But His coming again is in our future and we
'see' it only in part.

WEEK 7

Building love and holiness

Icebreaker

Who do you most want to be like? Think of a person you know (or knew) – someone you admire for who they are or were, rather than for their possessions, fame etc. Make a list of up to six qualities you admire in that person.

Bible Readings

- 1 Thessalonians 1:6–10 (imitators in love, faith, evangelism, serving God)
- 1 Thessalonians 4:1–12 (instructions on holy living and *agape* love)
- 1 Thessalonians 5:6–28 (life in Christ – key passage)
- 2 Thessalonians 2:13–17 (reasons to stand firm, entering salvation's fullness)
- 2 Thessalonians 3:4–16 (perseverance and obedience, not laziness)

Opening Our Eyes

This final week of our study on Thessalonians looks at morality, holiness, authority and correction. Heavy stuff – are you feeling condemned already? Actually, it's about welcoming 'the message ... with the joy given by the Holy Spirit'. In particular, we focus on faith, hope and love and 'turning to God from idols to serve the living and true God' – so it's 'turning to' more than 'turning from'.

Holiness makes us distinctive. Its root meaning is 'set apart', but this does not mean isolated from God and people – just the opposite. We're redeemed through Jesus' death and resurrection, given full access to love and to be loved by Him – and to let His life and love flow through us to others. None of us does this perfectly yet, any more than the Thessalonians did, but we're redeemed back into relationship with Him and so can grow in our capacity to allow His love to flow through us. He gives His Spirit, Scripture, people, faith and hope. And although some things we read in the Bible might seem a little 'heavy' and complicated, all – including holiness – distils to the simplicity of: '"Love the Lord your God with all your heart and with all your soul and with all your strength and with all your mind"; and, "love your neighbour as yourself"' (Luke 10:27). The Beatles sang that all we needed was love. However, the kind of love they had in mind was not quite Jesus' (or Paul's) self-giving, costly love that's kind and patient with everyone, warns the idle, encourages the timid, lives at peace with others, helps the weak – the kind that died for us. We can learn much from these passages in Thessalonians about the love that endures.

Although Greek and Roman gods were worshipped in the free-thinking, cosmopolitan Thessalonica of Paul's time, apparently they didn't mean much to most people. Some preferred mystery cults, others spent their spare time and energy in wild sexual activities. A number who subscribed to none of the above, though not Jewish, attended Synagogue, being attracted to the morality, the worship and to God. But, oh dear, the circumcision – and all those rules! As a result, many in this group of Gentiles responded to Christ when Paul preached. As we've seen, they excelled in faith, love, witness and faithfulness under persecution. Evidently, though, some still lacked self-control over matters that didn't build *agape* love – lust, laziness, gossip or divisiveness. Any individual or church will have some areas and attitudes that still need attention. When considering what you may need to personally work on, remember to do this with the Holy Spirit's help. He knows in what order we need to change and grow and He loves to help and encourage us. Remember, growing in holiness is often not so much 'turning from' but 'turning to' – from night to day, darkness to light, lust to love.

This is the last week of our study but not of our daily walk with and growth in God. That has its 'downs' and long slogs as well as its 'ups' – its times of real excitement and amazing growth. I pray that these studies will have encouraged you to see and hold onto all the good that God has given us – and that the nourishment you've received will continue to help build and sustain you and your churches within the love of God.

Discussion Starters

1. What ongoing difference does it make for you to '[turn] to God from idols to serve the living and true God' (1 Thess. 1:9)?

   _____

   _____

   _____

   _____

   _____

2. From where does Paul say authority ultimately comes? From whom do you learn and what's your attitude to those 'over you in the Lord'? Do any problems over authority or discipline in your church need prayer?

   _____

   _____

   _____

   _____

   _____

3. From 1 Thessalonians 5:11–22 and 2 Thessalonians 3:5, make a checklist of things to do with our relationship with: a) God and b) people. What's your weakest area in each? Encourage one another to grow God-wards in that area. Pray 1 Thessalonians 5:23–24 for each other as you agree to help over your respective weaknesses.

   _____

   _____

   _____

   _____

   _____

   _____

5. In what areas are you a model or example for others? Tell one another, as we tend not to see the good in ourselves!

_____

_____

_____

_____

_____

_____

_____

6. How do you grow in love?

_____

_____

_____

_____

_____

_____

7. 1 Thessalonians 5:8 lists some 'armour' God gives to help us live His difficult way of love, day in, day out – to 'endure'. Paul expands that list slightly in Ephesians 6:13–18. Can you share how it works for you to 'put on' or 'turn to' – the things of God? Things like faith, hope, love and truth.

_____

_____

_____

_____

_____

_____

_____

Personal Application and Seeing Jesus in the Scriptures

Fixing our eyes on Jesus is a good way to go, to grow and to build on the firmest of foundations! Three words that keep cropping up in Thessalonians, and therefore run through this study guide, are foundational too – they are faith, hope and especially love. Maybe a good way to begin to build ourselves and our churches up in those three 'things that endure' is to search the Gospels for instances where Jesus exhibited each one. And perhaps to notice how He avoided building on foundations which will crumble, such as unbelief, despair, hatred, or selfish lusts. Start reading – and noting. You'll see many examples, both negative and positive tools and 'building blocks' on almost every page. Ask the Holy Spirit to teach you how to grow in all of those things, to prompt you moment by moment, to strengthen and expand you so that you might become distinctively more like Jesus and attract others to follow Him, just as the Thessalonians did.

Leader's Notes

There's lots to read this week so, for the longer passages from Acts, choose a confident reader or two and think of them as Luke and his companions telling you their gripping story for the very first time. Or ask people to read the passages before you meet, along with the Introduction to this guide. Don't let the group become bogged down in details. Let the overall story speak – and what a story it is! Perhaps find a map of Paul's missionary journeys and point out the places mentioned. When reading the passages from 1 Thessalonians, ask people to focus primarily on what they reveal about: a) what happened and b) how Paul would be feeling as he dictated the words. Depending on time restraints and the nature of your group, you could find a different icebreaker and avoid the first question and the Matthew reading, if necessary.

I've included a number of readings and varied discussion starters each week. You might not fit all into the time available, so read them through beforehand and select those most appropriate to your group. The group may wish to further their study at home.

To help make sense of the Thessalonian letters, this week we're going to set the scene. For example, Paul's words in 1 Thessalonians 1:6–8 will witness even more to the power of the gospel – which is perhaps the most exciting and important thing that Thessalonians has to say to us.

It's important to recognise that Paul had been worried – and probably very discouraged. The same may well happen to us when we try to spread the good news about Jesus and help build up new (or even more mature) Christians in their faith. Such endeavours are seldom straightforward or without struggle. We'll see later that it wasn't all sweetness and light in Thessalonica either, so be sensitive to those in the group who express discouragement, even bewilderment – and to those who may have searching questions to ask of God. Jesus' parable of the sower shows what may happen when people begin to follow Him.

Setbacks don't diminish the power of the gospel. The Holy Spirit often intervenes in unexpected ways and at surprising times. I recall a time when a woman I'd never met before tried to thank me for something I'd apparently said to her at a dinner party that had caused her to start searching for God. Well, I had actually never attended this event, but my Christian friend had. Although she couldn't remember the conversation, clearly God had used something she'd said to crack open this woman's hard 'seed-coating' and soften her heart towards Jesus. You could ask if anyone has lost touch with someone they'd hoped to lead to Jesus, only to learn, years later, that the person had been found by Him. Remember, sowers aren't responsible for making seeds germinate.

Perhaps suggest that people read through both letters to the Thessalonians at home before meeting next time. (Reading eight short chapters, totalling 136 verses – five pages in my Bible – isn't onerous.) It helps to see not a string of verses but letters, part of a conversation held at a distance. Try and encourage the group to pick up the heart, the flow and feel of them. Sense the living relationship between their author and his first readers. Even though it all happened nearly 2,000 years ago, it comes alive – how amazing is that?

Week 2: Building tools: encouragement and thanksgiving

Today's study involves no difficult theology. It's practical and could well run deep, proving life and church-changing. The good thing is that anyone can choose to be thankful and to encourage others – and the more you practise the easier it becomes.

Alternative Icebreaker:

The most significant things that happen on the creative writing holidays I lead often have little to do with writing. For feedback each day we divide into groups of five or six, which become seen as a safe place within the larger group. Before the last day I mention that most of us receive far more discouragement than encouragement during our lives. I ask everyone to think of the person sitting on their left in the previous small group feedback session and come up with something to encourage them as a person, even more than in their writing. I suggest they might want to pray and ask God what to say, since they won't know that person very well. That half hour during which members of the feedback groups encourage one another often accomplishes more lasting good than all my hard work and input does.

You might like to try something similar with your group. Though it takes time, it will give practical, hands-on experience – and encouragement to encourage! Perhaps try it in the last 40 minutes or so of the session instead of at the start. Hand out a blank A4 sheet of paper to each member of the group. Ask them to print their name at the bottom of one side of this then pass it to the person on their left. All then turn the sheet over and, starting at the top of the blank side, write (legibly) a sentence of specific encouragement about the person whose name is on the other side. Then fold it over, as

in the game 'consequences', and pass it on to the left again. Repeat until the sheet arrives back with the person whose name it bears. Each person can then read it out to the group if they wish or simply keep and read it later. Take especial note of where the encouragement is consistent – probably a sign that it really does apply!

Recommended book

The beautifully written, inspiring *One Thousand Gifts* (by Ann Voskamp, mentioned earlier in this study) sees thankfulness as a tangible means of grace which becomes possible within very ordinary circumstances. The bit about thanksgiving (Ann Voskamp calls it *eucharisteo*) preceding the miracle is on pages 71–72 of my hardback edition (ISBN 978-0-310-32191-0). Available via the usual internet outlets as well as bookshops. Also as an e-book.

Week 3: Building on what kind of leadership and authority?

It might be good to start by everyone reading the Philippians passage. Encourage spoken prayers of praise to Jesus. Pray that He gives more insight into what can be vexed questions about leadership and followers.

Then you could divide into four groups, each of which searches quickly through the given passages. Each group could make a list in answer to just one of the first four questions, then share their list with the rest before you all continue with the rest of the study. When considering some of the later questions, feel free to draw on other scriptures within and outside Thessalonians.

In any kind of warfare, attacking leaders is an effective strategy. Church leaders are no exception. They face extra temptations that come with the role, including usurping or abusing of power which belongs to Christ alone, ducking responsibility and not exercising authority necessary for the health of the whole 'body', or becoming so over-responsible and 'driven' that they burn out. Pray for them – and for more leaders to arise.

Often church splits happen when different factions start supporting different leaders – providing a field-day for the enemy to bring everyone down. Again, watch and pray!

Here is some further material if your group would like to look further into the way Paul trained up new leaders. We'll start with Timothy. Paul visited the small town of Lystra twice. By the second occasion, Timothy's mother and grandmother had become Christians and Paul took young Timothy with him when he set off. Why? In 2 Timothy 1:5–6 Paul writes of Timothy's sincere faith and 'the gift of God, which is in you through the laying on of my hands.' Paul must have seen something in Timothy –

and Timothy must have wanted to follow Paul – perhaps relishing the thought of adventures to come. They did come, quickly! Though Timothy, unlike Paul and Silas, escaped flogging and imprisonment at Philippi, their first port of call. Perhaps, being so young, he 'slipped under the radar' and that was why Paul sent him back to see what was happening in Thessalonica later. Having heard that many had risen up against the new Christians in the town, Paul trusted Timothy to slip in, find out and report back accurately to him. Some training!

In 1 Corinthians 4:17 Paul called Timothy 'my son whom I love, who is faithful in the Lord.' Timothy's mission to Corinth wasn't a great success, yet he was the one to whom Paul handed over responsibility to carry on his own ministry after his death. If Thessalonians were among the first of Paul's letters, then those to Timothy were his last. Would you believe that Timothy's name is mentioned more times in the New Testament than anyone's other than Jesus, Peter and Paul himself?

Unusually we have only one name associated with the new church in Thessalonica – Jason, the man with whom Paul, Silas and Timothy stayed. He appears nowhere else in the Bible, other than in Romans 16:21, where Paul mentions a fellow countryman called Jason being present as he writes much later from Corinth. We don't know whether anyone else in Thessalonica might have heard the gospel or known the visiting evangelists previously, nor whether Paul established any leadership before leaving Thessalonica – it seems unlikely. But we do meet Macedonians and even Thessalonians who travelled with Paul – Secundus once in Acts 20:4 and, notably, Aristarchus, who is mentioned in Acts 19:29, 20:4, 27:2, Colossians 4:10 and Philemon 24. Paul was never a 'lone ranger' leader: wherever possible he recognised, worked with and trained up others.

Week 4: Prayer and the nature of salvation

First, read John 17 and ask people to look out for comparisons between that and Paul's prayers in the Thessalonian passages.

When exploring the third and fourth questions, as the group now know quite a bit about the background of what has been going on, ask them to imagine that they are Paul, writing to the Thessalonians. This might make it easier to see the raw honesty in some of Paul's prayers. There's nothing wrong with honesty – the psalmists do the same. If you're frustrated that you're being prevented from doing what you believe God has called you to, tell God about it! If you're hurt and perplexed about why 'your people' have become enemies, tell Him – then listen to Him. If you're confused, unsure of the way forward, wondering if you've been hearing God's guidance correctly; if worried about the health, physically and spiritually, of vulnerable people you love; if you are even beginning to wonder whether God is the powerful, victorious Saviour He says He is; if you're unjustly maligned by people who distort the gospel message you've communicated at such cost to yourself – tell God. Seek Him. Be open to whatever surprising thing He might do – this God who delights to bring beauty and new life out of ashes! And don't be afraid to ask others to pray for you – Paul does!

You might want to finish by praying over one another one or more of Paul's beautiful exhortation and blessing prayers from Thessalonians – I've copied several below – and then say the Lord's Prayer together. Make a habit of blessing one another in this way. Learn to receive such blessings too, and to let their truth take root deep within you:

'May your work be 'produced by faith, your labour prompted by love, and your endurance inspired by hope in our Lord Jesus Christ' (1 Thess. 1:3).

'May the Lord make your love increase and overflow for each other and for everyone else, just as ours does for you. May he strengthen your hearts so that you will be blameless and holy in the presence of our God and Father when our Lord Jesus comes with all his holy ones' (1Thess. 3:12–13).

'Rejoice always, pray continually, give thanks in all circumstances; for this is God's will for you in Christ Jesus. Do not quench the Spirit. Do not treat prophecies with contempt but test them all; hold on to what is good, reject every kind of evil. May God himself, the God of peace, sanctify you through and through. May your whole spirit, soul and body be kept blameless at the coming of our Lord Jesus Christ. The one who calls you is faithful, and he will do it ... The grace of our Lord Jesus Christ be with you' (1 Thess. 5:16–28).

May His power 'bring to fruition your every desire for goodness and your every deed prompted by faith ... so that the name of our Lord Jesus may be glorified in you, and you in him, according to the grace of our God and the Lord Jesus Christ' (2 Thess. 1:11–12).

'May our Lord Jesus Christ himself and God our Father, who loved us and by his grace gave us eternal encouragement and good hope, encourage your hearts and strengthen you in every good deed and word' (2 Thess. 2:16–17).

'May the Lord direct your hearts into God's love and Christ's perseverance ... may the Lord of peace himself give you peace at all times and in every way ... The grace of our Lord Jesus Christ be with you all' (2 Thess. 3:5, 16, 18).

Week 5: Dealing with difficult or contentious issues and misunderstandings

This week's study provokes big questions. Without time to tackle all six listed this week, decide which would be most helpful for your group and which to avoid for now. I find question 6 most important, because I've seen churches avoid seeking God's way through current issues – and so keeping people from Him. Other churches have split apart through ungodly disputes.

Questions 3 and 4. Don't speculate or argue too much about the end times. Remember that early Christians were suffering persecution. Letters could be intercepted and often include coded references hard for us to understand. If you read Matthew 24, point out that most of it probably refers to the fall of Jerusalem in AD 70. Perhaps Matthew 16:28 could be read as Christians seeing Jesus' kingdom in operation in greater measure after His Resurrection and the coming of the Holy Spirit – but, as it follows the verse about Jesus coming in His glory with all His angels, I doubt that explanation. Assure people that it's OK if their questions remain unanswered – these things are God's responsibility, not ours! Jesus said: 'You do not know the day or the hour' (Matt. 25:13).

Scholars have widely differing opinions about the meaning of the 'man of lawlessness', the rapture and other end-times references in Thessalonians. If you want to explore these passages further, I would recommend Tom Wright's commentary.[1] Taking modern biblical scholarship, together with insights into the culture and language of the time, Wright is clear, accessible, practical – and makes more sense to me than anyone else. For deeper, possibly life-changing insights into biblical teaching about what happens after death and after Jesus comes again, do read *Surprised by Hope.*[2]

Question 5. Don't devote a whole session to this! Though if your church has lots of new believers, someone may need to review any teaching programmes you have. Similarly for children's work – I've observed children learning through things such as: painting, modelling and acting like sheep! Think: what are the priorities in what should be taught, and how can you make it as engaging as possble?

Question 6. When I was at university the current work of the Holy Spirit was the big issue. A wise pastor in the town said, 'There's always something. A few years back it was Calvinism versus Arminianism. Before that Dispensationalism' (which involves the rapture, see 1 Thess. 4:17). Each generation, each decade, grapples with a different controversy; each seems all-consuming at the time. Truth is important, but not more important than Jesus. Or love. That's why it's best to keep bringing the discussion back to 'how did Paul deal with controversial or difficult issues?' Today's 'elephant in the room' I'd say is homosexuality – issues around it are splitting some churches, just as 'women in leadership' has done. These things won't go away if we ignore them. Neither splits nor 'heads in sand' show outsiders God's love. So, when considering how you as a group or church handle controversy, maintain love and respect for one another, humility for yourselves and Jesus at the centre. Think back and pray about anything ungodly that is a legacy of past controversies – and then think forward to what you can learn. I find John Donne's long poem 'Satire III' helps – it talks about some of the controversial issues of the time. Search for it online and read the 14 lines between 'though truth and falsehood be/Near twins' and 'mysteries/Are like the sun, dazzling, yet plain to all eyes.'

[1]Tom Wright, *Paul for Everyone: Galatians and Thessalonians* (London, SPCK, 2002).

[2]Tom Wright, *Surprised by Hope* (London, SPCK, 2007).

Week 6: Dealing with persecution, enemies and evil

The purpose of this week is to clarify our hope for the future and note godly strategies for dealing with such things as evil, injustice, suffering and enemies of the gospel – in whatever forms we come across them today. Being aware of God's strategy, 'His story', we'll pray with more understanding for His kingdom to come. But be prepared for a bumpy ride, emotionally and theologically. Remember that these letters were written to people under persecution, so references may be coded. For the Thessalonians persecution came mainly from local Jews, but several Roman emperors declared themselves divine, demanding worship – meaning trouble loomed for Christians in some very uncertain times. Tom Wright's commentary (op. cit. p.148) points out that Emperor Gaius Caligula mandated his huge statue be erected in Jerusalem's Temple and believers thought that, had he not been murdered in AD 41, 'the Roman–Jewish war of 66–73 might have started 25 years earlier.' That war led to the Temple being destroyed forever in AD 70. Many scholars believe both Paul and Jesus foretold that event as 'The day of the Lord' – perhaps layering other end–times meanings alongside.

Worldwide, more Christians have suffered terrible privations and died for their faith in recent years than during the rest of church history. Comparatively few who will read this book will have been exposed to such things. If we've not faced totally despotic and corrupt authorities ourselves, we may become agitated at the thought of persecution – would we withstand it? The standard answer is that God gives grace for what we need at the time, not for what we don't need. He also tells us not to worry about tomorrow, to trust Him, to pray for and help those who suffer – so try to keep the group focussed on those things.

For the first two questions (about 'enemies' and 'tools')
maybe share the given Bible readings between the group,
asking each person to note anything found within 'their'
passage. Remember that 'enemies' can be internal to each
individual. Then make a master-list on a big sheet of paper
or computer. Some powerful testimonies may arise through
sharing scriptures that have helped hard-pressed individuals.

Question 4: God says to Abram of the original inhabitants
of the Promised Land: 'In the fourth generation your
descendants will come back here, for the sin of the
Amorites has not yet reached its full measure' (Gen. 15:16).
God hardens Pharaoh's heart in Exodus (cf Acts 28:27;
John 12:40; Matt. 13:15 – referring to Isaiah 6:9–10).
Think also of Isaiah 5:20: 'Woe to those who call evil
good and good evil, who put darkness for light and
light for darkness, who put bitter for sweet and sweet
for bitter.' This I believe refers to those who'll receive
God's wrath (which means 'anger'). 'He will punish those
who do not know God and do not obey the gospel of
our Lord Jesus' (2 Thess. 1:8) does not mean, in my
opinion, those who've never met God, nor those who
disobey Him sometimes, but those persisting in sin and
utterly unwilling to submit to God. Some, convinced
they are greater than He and their ways more 'right',
set themselves up as judges, keeping others from Him.
Others allow themselves to become so totally deluded
and unrepentant, removing themselves so far from His
ways and His love that, if God's love and righteousness
are to prevail, His wrath and judgment become their
only possible end. For the rest, remember: 'The LORD is
compassionate and gracious, slow to anger, abounding in
love' (Psa. 103:8).

Week 7: Building love and holiness

Icebreaker:

Give everyone just five minutes to write their lists.
Qualities could be anything from humour or clear-
headedness to compassion. Then ask each to read them
to the group, without revealing the person admired.
Don't mention that you're going to do this beforehand
but when you hear qualities admired by the reader of the
first list and can see those same qualities in that person,
say so. Encourage others to do the same as you continue
round the group. This is an exercise psychologists use
and they've found it's astounding how nearly all exhibit
the qualities they admire in others. Of course, most of us
feel we fall so far short of our 'models' that we're utterly
unconscious of the fact and need others who know us
well to affirm us in those things.

For Christians it's encouraging to think that if it works
with people we admire, presumably the same applies if
we admire – and worship – Jesus. You might like to read
Hebrews 12:1–2, which seems to sum up much of what
we're looking at today, then spend a few moments in
silence, fixing your eyes on Jesus. 'Therefore, since we
are surrounded by such a great cloud of witnesses, let
us throw off everything that hinders and the sin that
so easily entangles. And let us run with perseverance
the race marked out for us fixing our eyes on Jesus, the
pioneer and perfecter of faith. For the joy that was set
before him he endured the cross, scorning its shame,
and sat down at the right hand of the throne of God.'

Discussion starter 1: Idols might be whatever we trust or
give primary worth (worship) to, instead of to God.

Discussion starter 2: Paul can sound a little harsh or even
overbearing sometimes in these letters over matters of his

own authority and of church discipline. Remember though that it is especially easy to lead very new Christians astray and it looks like this was happening. Some, perhaps the synagogue leaders, had tried to discredit Paul, assert their own authority and misdirect the people. Church leaders do need to exercise spiritual authority but it's very easy to abuse – church history is full of one shocking example after another. Try not to enter muddy waters here but refer to 2 Thessalonians 3:7 – leaders should be a good example and 'work hard' for their flock (1 Thess. 5:12). Scripture has plenty more to say on the subject, notably that godly leaders serve Christ and their flock rather than seek status or power for themselves.

As you reach the end you might want to review what you've learnt from this study. Including which God-given tools you can now use better to build up yourselves and your church in Christ – and to spread the gospel.

Notes …

Notes ...

Continue transforming your daily walk with God.

Every Day with Jesus

With around half a million readers, this insightful devotional by Selwyn Hughes is one of the most popular daily Bible reading tools in the world. A large-print edition is also available.

72-page booklets, 120x170mm

Life Every Day

Apply the Bible to life each day with these challenging life-application notes written by international speaker and well-known author Jeff Lucas.

64-page booklets, 120x170mm

Inspiring Women Every Day

Written by women for women of all ages and from all walks of life. These notes will help to build faith and bring encouragement and inspiration to the lives and hearts of Christian women.

64-page booklets, 120x170mm

Cover to Cover Every Day

Study one Old Testament and one New Testament book in depth with each issue, and a psalm every weekend. Covers every book of the Bible in five years.

64-page booklets, 120x170mm

Cover to Cover Every Day **is now only available as an email subscription or eBook**

For current prices or to order, visit **www.cwr.org.uk/store**
Available online or from Christian bookshops.

Journey through the Bible as it happened in a year of daily readings

Read through the entire Bible in a year with 366 daily readings from the New International Version (NIV) arranged in chronological order.

Beautiful charts, maps, illustrations and diagrams make the biblical background vivid, timelines enable you to track your progress, and a daily commentary helps you to apply what you read to your life.

A special website also provides character studies, insightful articles, photos of archaeological sites and much more for increased understanding and insight.

Cover to Cover Complete – NIV Edition
1,600 pages, hardback with ribbon marker, 140x215mm
ISBN: 978-1-85345-804-0

Latest resource

David - A man after God's own heart

Old Testament hero David was a giant-killer, inspirational worshipper and one of Israel's greatest kings - and yet he was also an adulterer and murderer. The Bible reveals it all to us, and there is much that we can glean from both his victories and mistakes to help us today.

72-page booklet, 210x148mm
ISBN: 978-1-78259-444-4

The bestselling *Cover to Cover* Bible Study Series

1 Corinthians
Growing a Spirit-filled church
ISBN: 978-1-85345-374-8

2 Corinthians
Restoring harmony
ISBN: 978-1-85345-551-3

1 Peter
Good reasons for hope
ISBN: 978-1-78259-088-0

2 Peter
Living in the light of God's promises
ISBN: 978-1-78259-403-1

1 Timothy
*Healthy churches –
effective Christians*
ISBN: 978-1-85345-291-8

23rd Psalm
The Lord is my shepherd
ISBN: 978-1-85345-449-3

2 Timothy and Titus
Vital Christianity
ISBN: 978-1-85345-338-0

Abraham
Adventures of faith
ISBN: 978-1-78259-089-7

Acts 1–12
Church on the move
ISBN: 978-1-85345-574-2

Acts 13–28
To the ends of the earth
ISBN: 978-1-85345-592-6

Barnabas
Son of encouragement
ISBN: 978-1-85345-911-5

Bible Genres
Hearing what the Bible really says
ISBN: 978-1-85345-987-0

Daniel
Living boldly for God
ISBN: 978-1-85345-986-3

David
A man after God's own heart
ISBN: 978-1-78259-444-4

Ecclesiastes
*Hard questions and
spiritual answers*
ISBN: 978-1-85345-371-7

Elijah
A man and his God
ISBN: 978-1-85345-575-9

Ephesians
Claiming your inheritance
ISBN: 978-1-85345-229-1

Esther
For such a time as this
ISBN: 978-1-85345-511-7

Fruit of the Spirit
Growing more like Jesus
ISBN: 978-1-85345-375-5

Galatians
Freedom in Christ
ISBN: 978-1-85345-648-0

God's Rescue Plan
*Finding God's fingerprints
on human history*
ISBN: 978-1-85345-294-9

Great Prayers of the Bible
Applying them to our lives to
ISBN: 978-1-85345-253-6

Hebrews
Jesus – simply the best
ISBN: 978-1-85345-337-3

Hosea
The love that never fails
ISBN: 978-1-85345-290-1

smallGroup central

All of our small group ideas and resources in one place

Online:

www.smallgroupcentral.org.uk
is filled with free video teaching,
tools, articles and a whole host
of ideas.

On the road:

A range of seminars themed for
small groups can be brought to
your local community. Contact us at
hello@smallgroupcentral.org.uk

In print:

Books, study guides and DVDs
covering an extensive list of themes,
Bible books and life issues.

Log on and find out more at:
www.smallgroupcentral.org.uk

Courses and events

Waverley Abbey College

Publishing and media

Conference facilities

Transforming lives

CWR's vision is to enable people to experience personal transformation through applying God's Word to their lives and relationships.

Our Bible-based training and resources help people around the world to:
• Grow in their walk with God
• Understand and apply Scripture to their lives
• Resource themselves and their church
• Develop pastoral care and counselling skills
• Train for leadership
• Strengthen relationships, marriage and family life and much more.

Applying God's Word
to everyday life and relationships

CWR, Waverley Abbey House,
Waverley Lane, Farnham,
Surrey GU9 8EP, UK

Telephone: **+44 (0)1252 784700**
Email: **info@cwr.org.uk**
Website: **www.cwr.org.uk**

Registered Charity No. 294387
Company Registration No. 1990308

Our insightful writers provide daily Bible-reading notes and other resources for all ages, and our experienced course designers and presenters have gained an international reputation for excellence and effectiveness.

CWR's Training and Conference Centres in Surrey and East Sussex, England, provide excellent facilities in idyllic settings – ideal for both learning and spiritual refreshment.